THE ROCK'N RESTORATION

THE FIRMLY FOUNDED SERIES

Core LDS Doctrines
Made Easy for Kids

Written and Illustrated by
David Bowman

"True doctrine, understood, changes attitudes and behavior"

- Elder Boyd K. Packer

Why The Firmly Founded Series?

Today's LDS children are amazing! Have you noticed? ☺
They come to earth with a pre-mortal fire of faith just waiting to be stoked. I believe they are ready to be taught the pure, core doctrines of our church… but still in the fun, visually-engaging language of children. **The Firmly Founded Series** parallels the first three lessons in the **Preach My Gospel** manual. Missionaries focus on these lessons because they are the foundational teachings of the Restoration, the Plan of Salvation, and Jesus Christ's gospel. Why not do the same with our "investigating" children?

I hope these books can be an invaluable tool in helping you teach these young, valiant souls…
or for anyone who still likes to learn with pictures ☺

God Bless,

David Bowman

ISBN: 978-162972-205-4
SKU: 5152253

Printed in China
R. R. Donnelley & Sons, Shenzhen, China
10 9 8 7 6 5 4 3 2 1

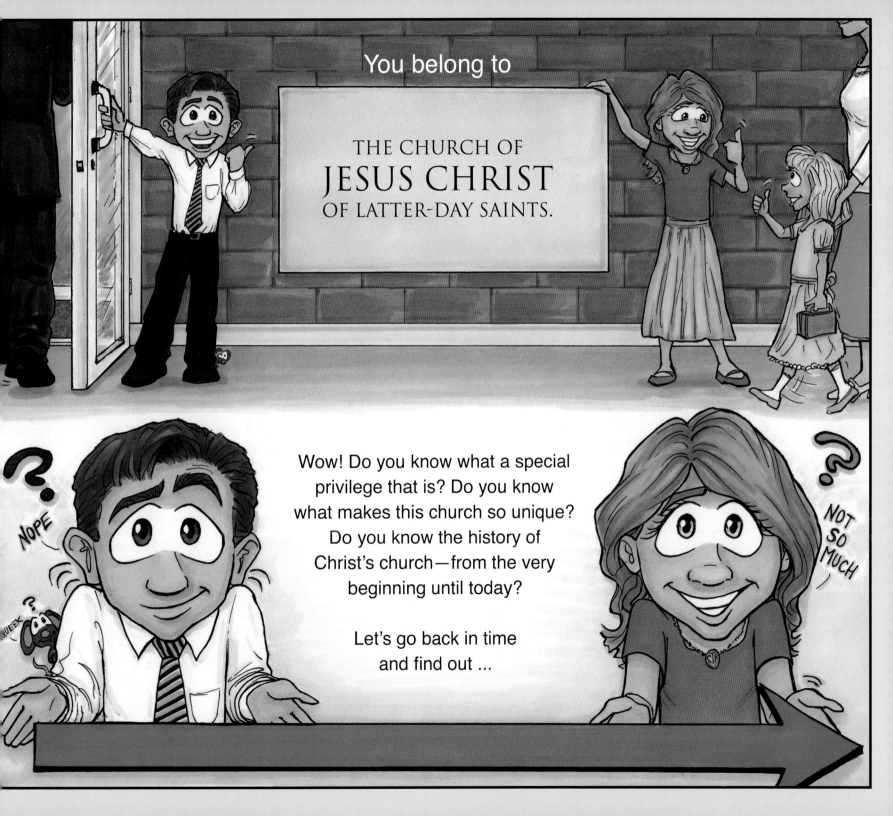

The Lord has always called **prophets**:

Adam, Moses, Isaiah, Nephi, Abinadi, Alma, and others. They were chosen men who received *REVELATIONS* from God. That means the Lord talked with them and they wrote those words down. We can read the words of the prophets in the Holy Bible and in the Book of Mormon.

HOLY BIBLE

THE BOOK OF MORMON

Another Testament of Jesus Christ

These ancient prophets wrote about a Savior of the World who would one day come and save us from death and sin.

They loved and worshipped Him, even though this Savior hadn't even been born yet.

And now, behold, I say unto you: This is the plan of salvation unto all men, through the blood of mine Only Begotten, who shall come in the meridian of time.

Moses 6:62

And I have a work for thee, Moses, my son; and thou art in the similitude of mine Only Begotten; and mine Only Begotten is and shall be the Savior, for he is full of grace and truth.

Moses 1:6

WE TALK OF CHRIST, WE REJOICE IN CHRIST, WE PREACH OF CHRIST, WE PROPHESY OF CHRIST, AND WE WRITE ACCORDING TO OUR PROPHECIES, THAT OUR CHILDREN MAY KNOW TO WHAT SOURCE THEY MAY LOOK FOR A REMISSION OF THEIR SINS.

2 NEPHI 25:26

I would that ye should understand that God himself shall come down among the children of men, and shall redeem his people.

Mosiah 15:1

THE SON OF GOD SUFFERETH ACCORDING TO THE FLESH THAT HE MIGHT TAKE UPON HIM THE SINS OF HIS PEOPLE... AND NOW BEHOLD, THIS IS THE TESTIMONY WHICH IS IN ME.

ALMA 7:13

But he was wounded for our transgressions, he was bruised for our iniquities: the chastisement of our peace was upon him: and with his stripes we are healed.

Isaiah 53:5

Years and years and years went by. Until one day ...

... He WAS born!

Jesus Christ was this promised Savior. He taught the people His gospel and showed us how we should live.

Jesus also established His Church. He chose 12 men to be His **APOSTLES**. They were to be "special witnesses" to tell people about Jesus and to lead His church. Jesus laid His hands on their heads to give them the **PRIESTHOOD**.

YES "FISHERS OF MEN"

The Priesthood is the power and authority to act in God's name ... such as to baptize or heal someone.

The time had come for the **Atonement**.
Jesus had the Last Supper with His 12 *APOSTLES*.

Afterwards, He took the *APOSTLES* to the Garden of Gethsemane where "He felt all that was sad, wicked, or bad ... all the pain we would ever know."* Then, wicked men captured Jesus and crucified Him on a cross.

(*"Gethsemane," by Melanie and Roger Hoffman)

Jesus Christ suffered all this for us because He loves us so much.

BUT, Jesus didn't stay dead for long. After three days, He was resurrected!

Jesus Christ's suffering and resurrection are what make it possible for us to repent, be resurrected, and live with God again. This is called the Atonement, and it's the most important thing that has ever happened. And the *APOSTLES* were there! They became "special witnesses" of Christ.

The resurrected Christ spent 40 days teaching His *APOSTLES* and then He ascended up into heaven. Before He left, Jesus commanded them to spread the good news of His Atonement all over the world.

WILL DO!

And that's exactly what they did!

Peter became the head *APOSTLE*, with James and John as his two counselors. The 12 *APOSTLES* taught Jesus' gospel to people all over. They baptized them into the church and gave them the gift of the Holy Ghost. They healed people. They gave the *PRIESTHOOD* to worthy men so they too could baptize and act in Christ's name. Peter and the *APOSTLES* received *REVELATION* from the Lord on how to lead the saints.

"Saints" is another word for members of the Church

And **The Church of Jesus Christ** grew! ☺

Eventually, people realized that something was wrong. They started reading the Bible and learning about Jesus. They felt inspired to form their own churches the best way they knew how. One by one, more and more Christian churches were created. This is called the **Reformation**.

Although these good men wanted to do the right thing, none of them had *PRIESTHOOD* authority to bring back Christ's first church. There were no prophets or *APOSTLES* called by Jesus Himself. There was no *REVELATION*.

The **ROCK** foundation was still missing.

So, the Americans fought a war with England and, with God's help, won that war.

They became their own nation ...
The United States of America. Yea!

After the war, our Founding Fathers wrote an "instruction manual" on how to lead their new nation. It's called the U.S. Constitution. It declares that everyone has religious freedom.

Through all of this, the Lord had prepared a free land for the return of His true church to the earth.

But who would the Lord choose to bring back His church???

Religious Freedom is the right to worship God however we want

But, the work of the Restoration had only just begun ...
Before he organized the church, Joseph was visited by an angel named Moroni
He showed Joseph where an ancient book of scripture, written on gold plates,
was buried. Through the power of God, Joseph translated
the gold plates into English.

This is why some people call us "Mormons" ... it's a nick name because of the Book of Mormon

THE BOOK OF MORMON
Another Testament of Jesus Christ

It became **The Book of Mormon: Another Testament of Jesus Christ**. Now the world had more scripture to teach us about Jesus Christ!

The Church of Jesus Christ of Latter-Day Saints grew quickly.

5 Finally, the saints built a beautiful city in Illinois called Nauvoo. There, they built a second temple. Inside that temple, the *PRIESTHOOD* keys Joseph had received were used to do sealings. That means families could now be sealed together for eternity! Woo Hoo! ☺ And, with these keys, the saints could also be baptized and sealed for those who had died!

1 The saints moved from New York to Kirtland, Ohio.

NEW YORK

KIRTLAND, OHIO

NAUVOO, ILLINOIS

MISSOURI

2 In Kirtland, they built the first **temple** in our day. Inside this temple, Joseph Smith was given the *PRIESTHOOD keys* to do some very special things.

3 The first missionaries went out to teach others about the Restoration.

4 Then the saints moved to Missouri, but were kicked out by a bunch of bullies ☹

"Priesthood keys" means "the right to do something," not an actual key

The church now had thousands of members. These new members were coming from all over to be with the saints in Nauvoo.

However, just as with the *early-day saints*, there were those who did NOT like the *latter-day saints*. They especially hated Joseph Smith.

One summer afternoon in 1844 ... Joseph, his brother, Hyrum, and a few of his friends were arrested and thrown in Carthage Jail. Suddenly, a large mob of wicked men attacked the jail.

They shot and killed Joseph Smith the Prophet, and his brother Hyrum.

It was a sad time for the saints. Would the church fall apart again like it did back in Peter's time? This time, the answer was NO! The apostle **Brigham Young** was chosen to replace Joseph Smith as the new prophet.

This became the Lord's pattern for His church: When a prophet dies, the *APOSTLE* who has been an *APOSTLE* the longest becomes the new prophet. When an *APOSTLE* dies or becomes the prophet, the prophet and other *APOSTLES* receive *REVELATION* and a new *PRIESTHOOD* holder is chosen to take his place.

This way the Church of Jesus Christ will never fall away again

Always **PRIESTHOOD** ... Always **APOSTLES** ... Always **REVELATION**.

Now, that's a **ROCK**'n foundation! ☺

Many more Latter-Day Saints came from all around the United States and England to be with the church in Utah. It was a hard journey. Some pioneers even had to pull their wagons with their own hands.

Many got sick and died. We are so grateful for their sacrifice.

LOGAN

AS WE DEDICATE THIS TEMPLE

SALT LAKE

SAINT GEORGE

MANTI

The Salt Lake Temple took 40 years to build!

During this time, the saints also built four beautiful temples in Utah. Yea! The biggest one was the Salt Lake Temple. Now, families could continue to be sealed for eternity. Now, the saints could continue to do temple work for their dead ancestors.

Since then, The Church of Jesus Christ of Latter-Day Saints has **grown and grown**. Brigham Young sent saints to settle more areas outside of Utah. Missionaries were called to go all over the world to preach the gospel. More temples were built. Church membership grew as more and more people were baptized and joined the church.

And the Lord continued to lead His church through many different prophets and *APOSTLES* ...

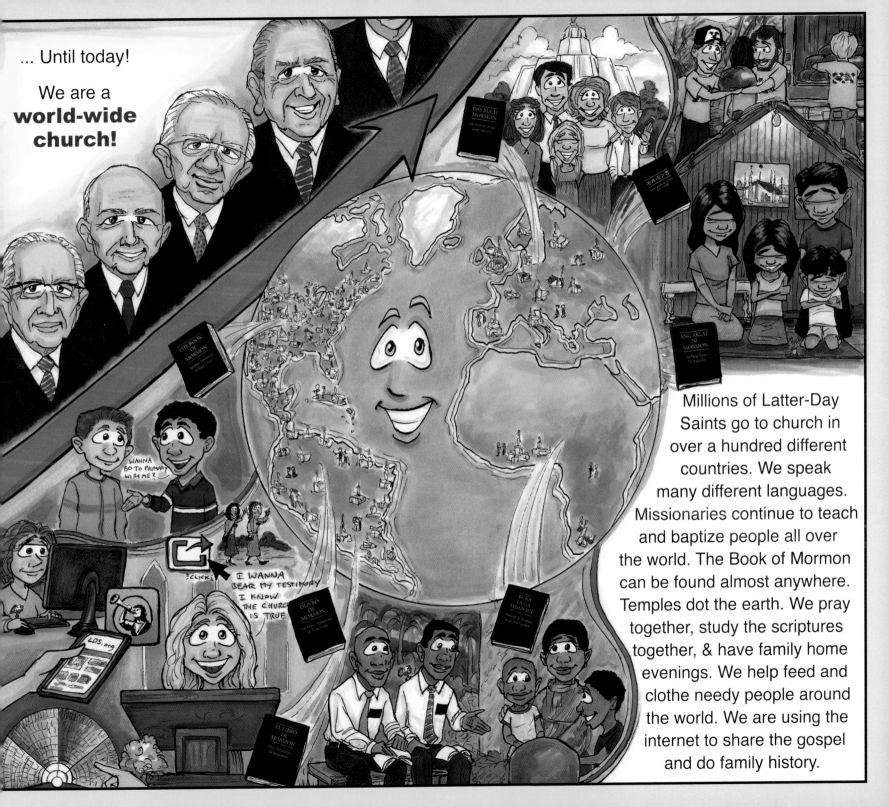

... Until today!

We are a **world-wide church!**

Millions of Latter-Day Saints go to church in over a hundred different countries. We speak many different languages. Missionaries continue to teach and baptize people all over the world. The Book of Mormon can be found almost anywhere. Temples dot the earth. We pray together, study the scriptures together, & have family home evenings. We help feed and clothe needy people around the world. We are using the internet to share the gospel and do family history.

There you have it! Now you know the history of Christ's Church:

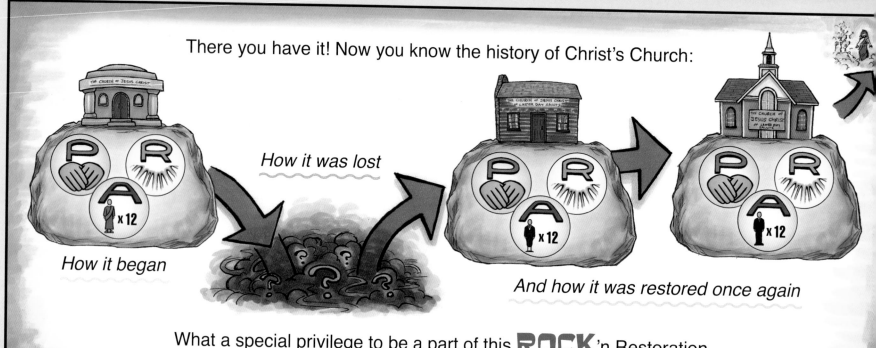

How it began

How it was lost

And how it was restored once again

What a special privilege to be a part of this **ROCK**'n Restoration.
All of the past prophets, *APOSTLES*, and saints are looking to our day.

What will **YOU** do for
God's Kingdom?

Great things,
my young friends, great things!

FHE Lesson Helps—The Rock'n Restoration

SONGS:

"We Thank Thee, O God, for a Prophet" Hymn 19

"Joseph Smith's First Prayer" Hymn 26

"Praise to the Man" Hymn 27

"The Church of Jesus Christ" *Children's Songbook*, 77

"Follow The Prophet" (esp. v. 9) *Children's Songbook*, 110

Children's Songbook, p. 86–89 (All good Restoration songs)

SCRIPTURES:

Need for **Prophets**—Amos 3:7

First Church, built on Apostles/Prophets—Ephesians 2:19-10; Ephesians 4:11-14

Great **Apostasy** foretold—2 Thessalonians 2:1-3; Amos 8:11-12

Restoration!—2 Nephi 27:26; DC 1:30; D&C 135:3

VIDEOS:

The LDS.org/media library is a treasure trove of great videos! Here are my favorites dealing with the Restoration. Just go to LDS.org and type in any of the following video titles (with the word "video") in the "Search" line:

The Great Apostasy (time: 16:33)

(Re-enactment of Wilford Woodruff's conversion story. Perfectly teaches how the elements of Christ's <u>first</u> church are found in today's <u>restored</u> church)

Joseph Smith-Prophet of the Restoration (13:09)

(Excellent summary of Joseph Smith's life, his key contributions, and his martyrdom. Remember to type in the dash "-", otherwise you will get the full, one hour movie that used to be in temple visitor's centers, which is also good!)

The Restoration (19:12)

(Full story of the First Vision)

What the Restoration Means for me? (4:44)

(Youth sharing testimonies at different church history locations)

The Message of the Restoration (2:22)

(Short "Mormon Message" with Elder L. Tom Perry testifying of the First Vision and the Book of Mormon)

QUOTES:

"I testify… that our Savior Jesus Christ is at the head of this Church, which bears His name. I know that the sweetest experience in all this life is to feel His promptings as He directs us in the furtherance of His work."

—Thomas S. Monson, "Looking Back and Moving Forward," *Ensign*, May 2008, 88

"Revelation and inspiration have come to [President Thomas S. Monson] in my presence, which confirms to me that God is honoring [the priesthood keys that the prophet holds]. I am an eyewitness."

—Henry B. Eyring, "The True and Living Church," *Ensign*, May 2008, 24

"This is the true Church, the only true Church, because in it are the keys of the priesthood. Those keys were restored to Joseph Smith, who then was authorized to confer them upon the members of the Quorum of the Twelve."

—Henry B. Eyring, "The True and Living Church," *Ensign*, May 2008, 20

"In New Testament times… and in modern times these (apostles) form the foundation stones of the true Church, positioned around and gaining their strength from the chief cornerstone, 'the rock of our Redeemer, who is [Jesus] Christ, the Son of God' [Helaman 5:12]."

—Jeffrey R. Holland, "Prophets, Seers, and Revelators," *Ensign*, Nov. 2004, 7

"Do you realize what we have? Do you recognize our place in the great drama of human history? This is the focal point of all that has gone before… The latter-day work of the Almighty, that of which the ancients spoke, that of which the prophets and apostles prophesied, is come. It is here. For some reason unknown to us, but in the wisdom of God, we have been privileged to come to earth in this glorious age."

—Gordon B. Hinckley, "At the Summit of the Ages," *Ensign,* Nov. 1999, 74

"You know no more concerning the destinies of this Church and kingdom than a babe upon its mother's lap. You don't comprehend it. It is only a little handful of Priesthood you see here tonight, but this Church will fill North and South America—it will fill the world.'"

—Joseph Smith, quoted by Wilford Woodruff, *Conf. Report*, April 1898, p. 57

ACTIVITIES/OBJECT LESSONS:

A ROCK'N FOUNDATION:

Find some building blocks or use paper cups (turned upside down). Refering to Ephesians 2:20, tell the kids we are going to build a church the same as Jesus' first church. Have kids start placing blocks/cups to form a base, identifying each block/cup as Apostles (you can use names), Priesthood, Revelation, and with Jesus Christ as the cornerstone. Once you have a solid base, start building upward in a pyramid fashion. These blocks/cups can be anything that is a part of Christ's church (baptism, gift of the Holy Ghost, sacrament, missionaries, seventies, etc.) Then explain how as the Apostles began to be killed (have kids take away one block/cup at a time from the base), the church collapsed (the Great Apostasy). But with the Restoration, have the kids rebuild the church with the same foundation/organization as the original church of Christ. Emphasize the need for the Priesthood, Apostles, & Revelation for the base.

FUN VARIATION OF THIS – Instead of blocks/cups... use people! Build a human pyramid, focusing on the same teaching points. Obviously, to do this you will need a large family or group. –OR- Better yet, Dad can get on all fours and be the "Foundation" of the church (with his four limbs being Priesthood, Apostles, Revelation, Christ). Have kids pile on his back as elements of the church. Then, one by one, take away Dad's limbs. ☺

TELEPHONE GAME APOSTASY

Play the classic telephone game. The more people, the better. Create a long, complicated sentence to start out with. After playing the game, make the connection how this is like The Great Apostasy: Like with the first person in the game, the original church of Christ was complete. But, little by little, person by person, important parts of the sentence were changed or left out (much like the long Apostasy period). So, by the last person, the sentence had parts of the original sentence but was not accurate or complete (much like the churches of Joseph's Smith's time).

FUN VARIATION OF THIS – Instead of doing this game with a sentence, act out charades. Send everyone out of the room but one person. Act out an entire made-up scene (with lots of details) for that person to watch. Then, let the others in one at a time. As each person comes in, he/she watches the previous person act out the scene, and then in turn acts out what he/she just saw for the next person. Remember, no talking! By the last person, it's pretty funny ☺

WHAT'S THAT NUMBER EXACTLY? *(Need for doctrinal exactness)*

Dad takes out his cell phone and tells the kids that they're going to call mom on her cell. Invite each kid to come up and take turns dialing a number or two. When you get to the last two numbers, Dad tells the kid "Why don't we just switch those two numbers? And then you can talk to mom." When they protest, play along with words like "Oh c'mon, it won't matter. We got all the numbers correct, we're just doing a slightly different order." Then, help them make the connection (no pun intended☺) that Christ's church is much the same way. In ancient or modern times, people can't just change a few beliefs or practices (Apostasy) and have it still "connect." His church needed to be restored exactly and completely. "One Lord, one faith, one baptism." (Eph. 4:5)

HOMEMADE COPS *(Need for authority)*

Have the kids draw and cut out their own sheriff's badges. If you have policeman paraphernalia, get it out, put it on, holster it, etc… tell the kids "Tonight, we are going to be cops!" Once you are all attired, get in your minivan/SUV and drive to a spot where you can park and watch cars go by. Tell the kids "We're looking for speeders." When you see a car that might be speeding, tell the kids "Got one! Let's go give him a ticket!" As you pull out and try to enforce the law, respond to the protestations of kids with "Well, why can't we? We have badges, we are enforcing public safety which is good, etc." Finally, help them make the parallel between the need for AUTHORITY from the state to enforce the state's traffic laws… and the need for PRIESTHOOD AUTHORITY (not just good intentions) to act in Christ's name. Then go arrest some ice cream instead! ☺

SWIVELING SIGNS *(Need for a 2nd scriptural witness)*

Have each kid cut out a piece of paper or cardboard into the shape of an arrow. Next, thumbtack their signs (or nail them, if you are brave) to a stake or piece of thick cardboard that resembles a sign post (be sure to use only one thumbtack or nail). Tell the kids to hold up their signs, so that they point towards the kitchen. However, show them that their arrows are not secure and can rotate so that they point in an entirely different direction. Ask them, "How can we make it so these arrows can't be rotated/changed?" Answer: Add a second thumbtack. Then, write the word "HEAVEN" on the sign and make the parallel with scriptures. With one book of scripture only (one thumbtack = the Bible), hundreds of different churches exist because people interpret the Bible to mean many different things (rotate sign so that the way to "HEAVEN" is pointing in any direction). But with Another Testament of Jesus Christ (2nd thumbtack = Book of Mormon), the truth is established and can't be changed (the way to HEAVEN points in one consistent direction).

Last thing … There is great power in memorizing Joseph Smith's First Vision account. Have fun memorizing this as a family. It will be invaluable throughout your kids' lives whenever they share the First Vision story with someone.

"I saw a pillar of light exactly over my head, above the brightness of the sun, which descended gradually until it fell upon me. … When the light rested upon me I saw two Personages, whose brightness and glory defy all description, standing above me in the air. One of them spake unto me, calling me by name and said, pointing to the other— This is My Beloved Son. Hear Him!"

(Joseph Smith—History 1:16–17).

About the Author/Illustrator

Following his service as a full-time missionary in the Philippines, David Bowman graduated with a degree in illustration from Brigham Young University. He has since served as a release-time seminary instructor as well as a counselor and speaker at numerous EFY conferences. His special love is making the scriptures come to life for young people.

David is the author/illustrator of the bestselling *Who's Your Hero? Book of Mormon Stories Applied to Children* series. His other books include *The Great Plan of Happiness*; *Dude, Don't Be a Lemuel: A Teenage Guide to Avoiding Lemuelitis*; and *What Would the Founding Fathers Think? A YOUNG Americans Guide to Understanding What Makes Our Nation Great and How We've Strayed.*

He and his wife, Natalie, and their five children live in Arizona.

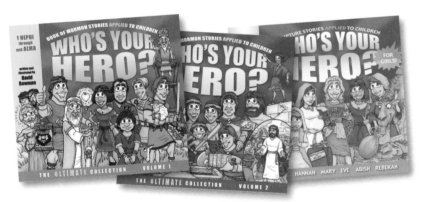

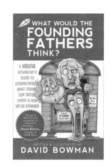

For Who's Your Hero? fun stuff, products, bonus material, etc. go to
www.whosyourherobooks.com

David Bowman is also the artist of the "Expressions of Christ" series. You can see his fine-art depictions of the Savior, as well as his other books, at
www.davidbowmanart.com